Gazza, the tragedy

JAN OSKAR HANSEN

ISBN: 978-93-6354-196-2

First Edition: 2025
Rs. 200/-

Cyberwit.net
HIG 45 Kaushambi Kunj, Kalindipuram
Allahabad - 211011 (U.P.) India
http://www.cyberwit.net
Tel: +(91) 9415091004
E-mail: info@cyberwit.net

Printed at Repro India Limited.

The Author

Jan Oskar Hansen is a poet, story teller and seafarer, born in Stavanger, Norway. He joined the merchant navy at 15 and spent most of his life at sea until settling in the early 90's in Portugal. His poetry has been widely published in hard copy and online, worldwide. Reviewers have generally commented that a love and honoring of living things stands out in Hansen's work, and deep humility; that it reveals with unflinching honesty man's shortcomings in his efforts to love, telling what there is to tell in a first person, deeply resident universal voice.

The poet is widely read and fluent in several languages, knowledge often acquired at night during his many years at sea. He chose to write primarily in English following enthusiastic reception of his work from English-speaking editors and readers.

His poems have been published in over 20 literary magazines worldwide, including:

Hudson Review, USA, Skyline, USA, Skald, Wales, La rue Bella, England, The Bards, England, War is a dangerous place, England, The Black Mountain Review, Ireland, ARS Poetica India, India, Metvere Muse, India, Poets International, India, Braquemard, England, Fvirefly Magazine, USA, Pphoo, India, Taj Mahal Review, India, Remark Magazine, USA, Journal Of Anglo-Scandianvian Poetry, England.

His poems appear in the following anthologies:

Shaken & Stirred (Bewrite Books, UK, 2003), Routes – Twelve Poets (Bewrite Books, UK, 2004), A Road Less Traveled (Bewrite Books, UK, 2005), Poetry from the Far Corners (Bewrite Books, UK, 2005), Listening to the birth of crystal (Paulapublishing, 2004) England, Peoplespoet 2 (Paulapublishing, 2005) England, The Review of contemporary poetry (Bluechrome, 2005) England, The book of hopes and dreams (Bluechrome, 2006) England.

Collections "Letters from Portugal" (bewrite books) Bristol, "La Strada" (Lapwing publishers) Belfast, "End of Voyage" (WFP. New York), "Marilyn Monroe remembered" Erbacce Press. Liverpool, "The Fairground" Ranchi India (out of print now).

Contents

A sonnet

In Gaza, Hamas has tunnels under Gaza
In New York, the Jews have built tunnels deep underground for a reason many find eccentric
I do not think when the world explodes in a nuclear war, some Jews are sure to survive
When the deed is done, and the stench of death
has evaporated, and the olive tree leaves look
like camouflaged Hamas, eternally crossing
a field blast tuned sand into gold
the New York survivors will find their way to
Jerusalem, trying to find a stone, if nothing else of the wailing wall.

The Vegetarian

I made a vegetarian meal the other day and recalled the days of yore when I wanted to become a veggie chef.
At the same time, I thought of changing my name to Peter since it sounded more long-term healthy.
I took the night train to Oslo, took nine hours on third class, and had a hard seat for a night,
but thanks to the blanket used as a tent
and somehow survived.
When arriving, I had a coffee at the cafe stations cafe, fell asleep but was woken up by a sure voice
that wore a uniform, telling me I was a tramp
and to get the hell out.
Oslo was an entirely gray town,
the roads, people, and houses were as if all colors had left town
and fled to Trinidad for the rest of the year
Standing at a corner, with a rolled up blanket in Karl Johans Gate,
the street leading up to the castle, the home of the king when he is not on his farm, I had lost interest in vegetarianism
found a proper working-class cafe and ate bacon, eggs, fried potatoes, and sausages as the cold sun shone over a miserable town
spent my money on a train ticket first class
back to a town with a frozen lake

Automobile industry

At the seaside, the water signaled many colors
pale sober gin, dark hue, then bottle green and pink like a nursery rhyme
no one took notice the sea was warning of a disaster.
It began in the late afternoon when the sun felt tired but hesitated to sink beyond the horizon
So much more to see, and the night lasted to six in the morning.
The cars by the seaside started all at once and
headed towards the bay and into the sea
the bottom of the bay was smooth, many cars were able to drive
far before they drowned, but the battery light lasted a long at
night, the bay was lit up like a gigantic stage for an opera
Shall we guess, Rusalka? An Italian opera
A water nymph in love with the human world and discovers her sexuality.
There was no way to stop this mass exodus
more and more cars flung themselves into the water in the bay;
yes, even patrol cars revolted
and motorized transport came to a halt
when motorcars had gone, it was the motorbikes turn to to headless drive into the sea
An island was born
when seabirds had fertilized the islet traffic
cones appeared together with of one way drive
no parking zones and zebra crossings
The world cried out for Elon Musk to come and sort out the problem
in the meantime, a donkey farm in the north of
Guarda, a hill top town near the Spanish border, made a roaring business renting out their animals.

Humanity

I looked up the Wikipedia to see if a man I had known for thirty years but never met was there. Do not exist, was the answer. I wrote my name also; it appeared I didn't exist either. I did once when thinking it was important, but some ladies
in Jerusalem had deleted me.
The ladies in Jerusalem are dedicated to keeping the holocaust alive, a hopeless case, all holocausts and there have been many forgotten. Right now in Palestine, there is low-level extermination going on, but since the perpetrators are people who suffered much, we pretend not to see.
As a man in an illegal settlement said:
We killed Jesus and are proud of it,

A sonnet

In Gaza, Hamas has tunnels under Gaza
in New York, the Jews have built tunnels deep underground for a reason many find eccentric
I do not think when the world explodes in a nuclear war, some Jews are sure to survive
When the deed is done, and the stench of death
has evaporated, and the olive tree greens look
like camouflaged Hamas, eternally crossing
a field blast tuned sand into gold
the New York survivors will find their way to
Jerusalem, trying to find a stone, if nothing else
of the wailing wall.

Unter den Linden

I have a soft spot for the German language
when a toddler, I had free access to a military camp where they had enormous horses and let me sit on top of one of them
(looking up horses,
I think they were Belgian draft horses)
Since I was 5 years old at the time, I reserve the right to be wrong
My mother said I could speak a little German
I don't think so, but when the Brits and the Americans came, my few words of German were too soon forgotten.
In the late fifties, I was onboard an old ship that
had survived the war but needed its motor seen to in Bremerhaven
the town bore scars of the devastating war
but there was full employment, and everyone was doing something worthwhile, like the farmer who took
took food scraps from ships and fed them to his pigs later, sold for slaughter through ship-chandelier to the merchant ship.
No, Bremenhaven was not Unter den Linden
Not a tree left, cold had the aftermath been
It was spring walking along streets where people sat out telling stories and laughing.
There was a sense of comradeship that made me feel the trauma they had gone through.
At that time, there were no beggars, and no one was following me around in the hope of getting some coins, which was annoying in places like Kingston in Jamaica and other places
Germany has not hitherto played the leading role
a great nation in Europe, this is because the burden

of the Holocaust, a burden unfairly put on the Germans alone to
bear, is coming to an end,
also, I think so is the headless policy of not being critical of
Israel's policies, which makes many countries
guilty of aiding and abetting the genocide of
of the Palestinian people

the winter of discontent

It was getting cold, my dog moved from the cool hallway to the corner sofa, a matter of reality
time to light the fire.
Our summer had a long time; we forgotten it does get cold in the Algarve.
I remembered a painting of the sinking sun, olive trees green as old gold, the mule on the road had eyes of onyx, and the sky was pink to please my childish heart.
Oh, levity; this is not the time!
The man who delivered wood neatly cut fitting the oven had a stroke, and the son had his father packed off to an old people home.
I remembered his son, so unlike his kind father,
a greedy, sniveling twat who obviously hated his father's natural dignity.
There are times when the apple falls near a tree and is picked up by a hex that alters the apple's perception the core is rotting, but the outside of the apple shines.

The son rang, he told me I had to buy more wood this year to save him a double journey, it would cost more this year as the price of petrol had gone up.
I did not ring him back, although he rang a few times, didn't answer the call because I did not care listening to the voice of hectoring greed.
When the firewood was used, I drove around the abandoned campsite and found leftover pieces of planks I cut up and used as fire.
In the waning days of February, before spring broke out and the

winter projected its last breaths of winter
I burned my poetry collection I had paid for printed in India
the books had not been edited
therefore an embarrassment, a statement of failure
still, it is not easy to burn your own books.
However, I spared a few books because I could see their value,
now spend my time busy
rewriting poems, I think does not deserve to die

Forgive the forgotten

I received the post from someone anonymous
a video, not knowing who had sent it, I put the video in a drawer
where it languished for years
Yesterday, when clearing up the drawers on my desk
full of copy pens that didn't work a broken
camera, seven pairs of shop-bought glasses, and a copy
paper, although I have no typewriter, and the video
the video showed how my life was when young
and the people I knew were young as well
play, anger, love, dance, and greed it was all there
nothing spared the blushes.
Watching the video many times till late at night
when it struck me, of all the people shown, I was
the only one alive and had moved on and left my youth behind
me; I felt a deep shame, a regret that
had not thought about them, those who had played
such a big part of my youth.
Later in the night, the forgotten floated up as pieces of a puzzle
that made no sense.
A fair girl, why did he behave so beastly towards her? A broken
stem of a wine glass was it his blood or someone else; a cre-
scendo of uncurbed rage.
The sudden darkness, a new dawn far away, where
dreams become alive, replacing the embryo that
died before life, entering the state of oblivion, yet what once was
exists in dreams and memories of those who once loved and
made life bearable

A Warped Tree

Today, when not arguing with Walter the Jew
on Facebook or Twitter
the ambiance in the house was surprisingly calm since I got a key
to my study in peace to read my latest collection
and found, at times, the poems had an internal rhyme and were
little stories
The pity is, I have to write without a publisher and
can't afford to hire one, those I dare to ask run a thousand miles,
one of them a poor man, is a lecturer in Udevalla
Last year, I visited a crooked tree so shy its roots curled in
bashfulness, and its leaves took an autumnal color. I wanted to
know if there was a way for me to help get her more gracious
and straight
She took offense and said she was 105.
I felt like pointing out the tree by the drive into our village -an
olive tree-is so old there is a possibility Jesus sat under it report-
ing protest notes to
the priests in the service of the Roman church
One day the came, the uncouth people from the traffic division
chopped down ancient history and threw the remains down a
drain.
Angrily, I protested to my doctor about the vandals
with my fist hit the table so hard a stethoscope fell to the floor,
and then the porter came,
and I was made to leave.
When I came to Portugal, the natural thing was to study and
learn the language, but at the time I was wrapped up learning
English

The Portuguese language is superbly fitted to Fado
but as a "lingo" for conversation, I fail, but
I knew enough to get married.
The Norwegian vocality sounds like a Dane
trying to talk Swedish and is like wet cement being poured down
a ditch dug by Lusitanos, spitting tobacco.
Ach, mein lieber Gott, I have lost many
friends in the last sixty years.

Ashdod (Israel)

This was a long time ago when Mohammad Morsi
was president of Egypt, a man loved by the people
That didn't cut the ice he was disliked by the USA
and hated by Israel; soon thenceforth, there was a coup
General Si Si became a dictator
A dictator is not so bad if he belongs to the right side
he did; the Israelis liked him, and so did the USA.
Two stern men (immigration) came looking at our
passports, clearly enjoying their status as new masters
The captain told me to line up the crew outside his office, where
the two men were handing out money, telling us not to talk about
the cargo
Naturally, I refused to accept the money
I wanted to why? Stern men issued threats and called me a
communist, until our captain said: for god's sake, Jan, take the
money so we can proceed.
Later in the afternoon, the ship Chandler brought
two crates of oranges, I insisted on checking the fruit
before taking them onboard
Lovely looking oranges on the top of the crates underneath most
were rotten, I refused to take them
this time, I was called anti-Semitic.
From the bridge, the captain hollered down to me
for god's sake, Jan, take the bloody oranges
or I will never hear the end of it
These days, Egypt was brokering a deal with Israel
but then the slaughter in Gaza happened
Whatever the deal was, it is put on hold for now

Der Spiegel

In Kashgar, where the Silk Road begins
I bought an apricot and saw a young
Fidel Castro on a bike
The woman who sold the fruit wore
a red shawl over her shiny black hair
knotted under her chin, a yellow silk
silk dress
do you see this man on a bike, I told
to the woman who sold fruit by the road
he is Fidel Castro of Cuba and is a very
famous man except in the USA.
Kashgar is the biggest outdoor market
in the world
Europe is puny, colorless and far away
why was Fidel doing in Kashgar
so far from Cuba.
I tell you, he is looking for a tobacco dealer
to supply him with Havana Cigars
Langley is too close to Cuba
A longer Silk Road is being built
with pipelines and trains to Hamburg
famous market of whores selling flesh
from dimmed rosy lit rooms.
If you want to buy a peach, you have to go
to Kandahar, or make a movie.
The man on the bike was a secular pope
his enemy tried to murder him for sixty years.

Born Bad

It is a hell of a war for many soldiers, but some of them thrive
and know how to survive and let others do the dying
it is also sexy, running in shot-up streets and ruined buildings,
firing into glassless windows in case the enemy might be lurking
inside
what they manage to kill are mostly panicked, weaponless
civilians and children in their cribs
For many soldiers, war is a perfect time to kill for free and be a
hero who, in peacetime, can be classified as a sociopath
For Jonas Mull joined the army and found a home
a structure to his life of bullying people, now he could
be a hard man and applauded,
in Falluja -Iraq-his reputation was cemented,
When a wounded Iraq soldier cried out in pain, he shot the
wounded and said: This should make him quiet!.
When that war simmered down, he was sent to what is called the
stateside and was made full sergeant because the officers in
charge thought he was a killing machine
effective when directed but less so when on his own
when his patrol got attacked, in the melee, he was partly shielded
by a lesser soldier, who
if wounded fell and was rescued by our sergeant.
There had been rumors about him liking you boys
this was overlooked, seen as an unmarried man
being fatherly
but something scandalous happened
we don't know what it was, but we can make an educated guess
He was sent back to the States, given the highest order

a non-commissioned officer can receive and be dismissed from his beloved army.
With his pension and savings from his army days, he
settled in Florida for the quiet life, and for the first time in his life,
he met a woman who was not a prostitute
with his- woman- he was settled for a while
but his sociopathic tendency began resurfacing
His girlfriend sensed this and moved out.
For a while, he was involved in brawl in bars
the police warned him more of this, and they would have to
arrest him despite his war record.
One day, he left for Mexico; rumors had it he got
a job as a bodyguard for one of the kingpins
that might be true he was a man who could not overcome the evil
that had taken abode in his soul

A tree in love

By the old road, before it meets a widened way
in a nearby stand two trees close together
we can see they are related
yes, mother and daughter
The mother, although taller, leans on her daughter
They are a refugee from a forest fire which they survived
only to get the news all trees had to be chopped down
to give space for a golf course.
A night after much rain had made the soil soft, they got the roots up and moved along the land,
near the road
The hope was to meet a group of woods and seek sanctuary, but now, an impasse.
The daughter said, we must let our roots grow under the road until it breaks down and traffic stops, and when the road is repaired, we can sneak over
We have to move fast, in ten years' time , we should be able to cross.
The two trees were well-liked in the forest hood not, complaining when birds made a racket
in summer made the ground cool, for rabbits.
They and moles, which usually made a home in trees' roots, went to work softening the oak the trees were trying to cross
The foxes chipped in, promising not to hunt at that
part, near the road, and warn other foxes to stay clear
If you wonder why the foxes were friendly, because on a cold, foggy winter night, a fox was lost and hunted by dogs, an oak tree said come hide in my hollow, and that saved the fox's life that lived a long life, a wise reynard, other foxes went to see when they need advice.

Everything was read in 10 or 15 years,
the young tree and her friend she telepathically meet to entwine
her roots with his, but her mother hesitated
She, the old lady, was fond of the clearing near the main road, so,
much more to see than being stuck in a forest
She also claimed the afternoon sunlight was good for her bark,
and her foliage was greener than before
The moles and other burrowing animals sensed the young tree's
distress and continued digging tunnels.
Years later (three's time), a man with a new ax walked
by the old tree, trying out the ax's sharpness chopped
off a few tree branches and nodded to himself yes, it's sharp
This incident was witnessed by the daughter, who woke up her
mother, who had been asleep at the time and told her
and said, we better move the mother poofoyed this and
they continue to stay near the main road.
Until the country had an economic collapse
and people
could not pay the heating bills

The man with the sharp ax had a dream a horse with wings flew
him to the clearing by the road, yes, he remembered that tree, the
heating-the-house, problem was solved
Rain began, and heavy rain lasted for weeks
tilling the soil into a soggy mess and the tunnels generations of
moles and rabbits
had made, a section of the road collapsed
Enabled the two trees to drag up their rots and sprint
across the opening and settle in the middle of the forest where
the daughter tree could mingle with her friend
and mingling of roots could begin
The country needed many workers to repair the road
this was seen by the economists as the beginning of good times
again, and strikes and civil war were avoided.

Winter in Cascais

This is a cold day, and bleak too, like a fish left behind
on the grass verge when the anglers go home for lunch
Sport fishing doesn't mean you want to eat the prizes
She is having salmon to day at the cafe on the first floor of our building,
I, when a farm boy in Norway, was served salmon or trout every day except Sundays
will settle for a slice of ham, boiled potatoes and salad
Olive oil is used here in Portugal, but I think food taste better with butter.
So, said the great chef and entertainer who hung himself
with towel hooked to a doorknob; his death tells us how little we know of other people's suffer, that can go so much deeper than we pedestrian folk can imagine.
Food doesn't mean so much anymore I eat because of annoying diabetes, but the healthy appetite has gone
The cafe serves a glass of good red wine with lunch
I like wine, but can only drink the red verity, that's OK,
I can live with this handicap and not feel prejudiced
On blue tainted days, the best thing to do is to it indoors
and read a favorite book, a good book can be reread several times when coming to pages know and agree with the writer on, and together laugh with the author

the vital moment

The great Greenland explorer, a giant of a manhis plane had
landeded, he was walking up the steps to the restaurant and
press waited
carrying his own bag and he was ninty five
at the top of the steps he stopped paused and collapsed, died.
The man had had a great life, it was the pause
at the steps that bothers me, did he, in a flash
see his own life, whether he had been a fraud
or let the people, he loved down, did he recall
the moments when failed them and himself
gripped fear, fighting his instict to runaway?

the eagle an an owl

A crow and a sparrow had painted themselves in daring colors
to appear masterful and became friends, both suffered from
bombastic self -believe, made a pact to kill an aged eagle
By doing so, they made life a misery for lesser birds that needed
an impetus to make fancy flying a daring adventure
clipped their wings and took up biking down steep slopes
and narrow boulders, with the added risk of breaking tails
A call went out to find an eagle that could fly higher and nearer
where the sky ended in a velvety arch
Hidden in a cave there was a young male eagle with a wide
wingspan able to impose the low on the glorious sky over
Alentejo, to keep order, alas, needed a lady eagle since there
wear none left, settled for a lady owl, who, as we know
can teach an eagle a thing or two
Together, the pair made life lesser birds exciting and, in time
produced a new type of eaglets never seen before

The singer

Elvis was not dead, he had been up the mountain
living on berries, playing hibernating with bears
and had become a vegan.
Elvis was now thin, his suit hanging like a haversack
in a ranch of starving horses
his suede shoes were too big, and his golden lame suit
hung loosely on his emaciated body.
Elvis decided to have a farewell concert and his voice
was the same Colonel Parker didn't think it was smart
Young people wanted to see other young people, not an elderly
gent, who could sing like Elvis.
Few people showed up and thought it was an illusion
Bill Clinton came but left early friends who had
an island had been found dead in his cell also he had
forgotten his saxophone.
Elvi sang a couple of songs, looked at the audience
said, Go Fuck Yourself, walked out and took the bus
to the mountain and his bears, and no one saw him again.

the dilemma

a man walking home from work through the Olivera noticed
a group of hanged men, who when alive, had argued
about the price of aceite
The devil, that had caused this, sat on a felled tree
polishing his hoof and sharpening his scythe
The man, who was on Sundays a lay preacher, was upset
and said what the devil are you doing?
the devil stopped sharpening his scythe, lit a cigarette
the tobacco aroma was intense in the still night
having inhaled a few times and the glow of his cigarette
made mystic circles in the dark
finally, he stumped out the fag with his hoof, cleared
his throat and said:
My job is to collect the souls of those who have trespassed
broken the law of nature, alas 20.000 thousand people
of the wrong sort were killed by those whose souls I was
to collect but could not
it was pointed out to me they were God's chosen people
Therefore, beholden to a promise I had made when God and I were
carving up the world, I could do nothing
Ok, I see, but what about the men in the Olivera?
As I was walking past, they were talking about football!
Would you believe it? I told them to go hang themselves, and they
did

Broken dreams

Tonight, I'm happy and sad
I refuse to cry over lost friends
I'm drunk too
It feels good to put the anchor of sobriety
let alcohol give wins to my sail
I am a clipper buying tea in China
not useless toys
Sleek my lines, women admired me
Let the clipper sail!
I don't care anymore
I will stay as long as I want
and make love to you
I'm sorry I left you, My Liverpool girl
I went to Brazil to harvest coffee beans
To Guatemala, I got there by chance
the beach in the moonlight
No, I have not forgotten my promises
One day more, only one day more
the ship always sails to other shores
I never had the time to write
the poem of my life

A letter to Sweden

Every year, I say, Come August, I will travel to Sweden
but when I go to buy a ticket, the price has gone up and
I decide to wait until next year.
Once, I met a girl in Stockholm who spoke a beautiful
Swedish, it was clear the Swedish language is as
beautiful as the Italian language, even more, I think
melodious, like listening to classical music without attitude
When August had gone, it had been quite rainy
Came September with soft sunlight and easy breaths
now that the fall was upon us, it was suddenly spring
to fit in with the April season's lambing.
"The rain in Spain falls mainly on the plane."
Not in my vale, we see pregnant clouds hasting by
shedding their load where it is needed, like in the bay
of Cascais
the flowers that grow in this surprise spring have
demure colors, less demonstrative, like saying
Don't, get carried away, we have done this before
Despite all this beauty, war is breaking out like
old plaque waking up to strike terror again
this time, Yemen is being bombed by the usual
criminals who have to safeguard the price of oil
In Yemen, where spring has been absent for years
one wonders, has there ever been a spring
in that poor, misbegotten country, yet her people
are heroic, trying to strike at the heart of Zionists
who have made our world a scary place that
can, due to our cowardice, see the end of the planet
as we knew it, which remains me this time if
there is a September I will try to meet that girl in Stockholm

the love bug

This, is my last letter
I have loved you from the first we met
Something about your eyes
the kindness of your heart
you know, if you can explain love
then there is no love, only acquaintances
you are going on a long journey
That's OK, I do understand
When you return, I will not be here
I just wanted to tell you how much I love you
how much I enjoyed your nearness
The aroma of your body when teasing me
with your youth and my old age
my hope was to be near you, nothing more
A dulcet dream of the unobtainable
Love is a rainbow, alas, where it falls
there is no crock of gold
Goodbye, my darling, thinking of you
Eases the burden of old age

Municipal bill

driving down from my eyrie, I write to sound learned
while the extent of my education was as a cook in the merchant navy
often thrown ashore in mystic harbors as a fabulist
I thought since there is no proof of god's existence and regarded
among the intellectuals as a pass time Subject
I still would like to know who is in charge of rainbows!
I, like to know, if he is an artist, why he uses the same colors
last time I checked. there were seven, perhaps a broader spectrum
will living things up like a weekly show at six o'clock
I once saw a rainbow, soaking wet, over a waterfall and miserable
and since it just hung there, it had no ending, and therefore lacked
the promise of economic bliss,
I sent Elon an email the other day kidding him, he took offense
you see, he found the crock of gold all by himself, and now
he is trying to find something worthwhile to do with his spare time
At the bottom of that hill, I crossed a bridge beyond the land
was sparse and dry, the few Palestinians were allowed to live in tents
providing the wore traditional dress when tourists came around
they were the rest of a nation stolen
and the people
eradicated, but the few who survived were taken good care of
I had forgotten the water bill on the mantlepiece, just as well
one day, the war will be about water.

The Quadro

When she left, it was late in the evening
on the snow-covered path to the street
her footprints were not visible
In the road, there were too many
footprints to recognize if any of them
belonged to her
years like layers of wood stacked up when
I saw her in a painting by Paula Rega
So many suffering women abused by men
and their desire to be loved, causing them
to fall into hardship
They survived while I suckled on a nipple
another woman, risking her future in
the hope of love where there was none
the endless poverty doing others' laundry
hands red bloated a ring of promise, not
kept, impossible to remove.
these are the women who do not leave
footprints in the snow
Paula Rega gave them a voice, reduced
the men, who had lost what they thought
was love, to fear ghosts in the longest night

1948

Israel declared statehood, the West was happy
the Jews had suffered and deserved a state
the fact that 700 thousand Palestinians lost
their homeland was overlooked.
We were all pro-Israel back then and thought
the Jews would usher in peace and prosperity
it was not to be!
We see the Israel of hope has turned violent
it wants more Jordan, Lebanon, Syria, and they
appear unstoppable and protected by the USA
can overlook the world's disgust.
Because of Israel's intransigence, new groups
like Hamas and the Hezbollah are dedicated
to end this Hebrew death cult of Israel.
In power now are the Zionists, who are hellbent
sensing and killing everything in their way
The Palestine people (40 % cristians) have
suffered cruelly at the hands of those we came
from the devasted Europe to find a new life
alas, they also had hatred in their hearts
and, as always, the innocent pay the price.
We, the people, what can we do?
We can stop buyin Israelly product and stand
firm against those who tell us we are
anti-Semitic a stigma we must bear with
fortitude

War today, Holywood tomorrow

As he sank into the deep sea, pellucid
fish ignored him, as did unsightly shrimps
the tempestuous insects of the ocean
As he sank deeper- less life- but the life that was were strange,
ghostly, and grotesque
for eyes not trained to see that the ugly can be beautiful
A ship sank; it was 1944 above, and the war raged the captain on
the bridge gave an order to his third mate who had lost his
uniform, showing a skeletal body
The captain dislikes this display proper dress on my bridge he
used to say, and clean fingernails are important
So are shiny black shoes.
The rest of the crew has gone walkabout,
they liked this new aquatic world better
than the war fought on the surface of the sea
A boy found a funnel of whirling air, entered one shot to the
surface, where a wave washed him ashore to a pristine beach
suitable for shooting a war movie.

Middle States

Was it Iwa, a beautiful state with rivers and lakes that Trump
won 50%of the votes, or was I wrong it might have been Idaho,
where great spuds are grown
and that is the problem this vast expanse of land in the heart of
America, yet unknown to the many who
think America is New York and Los Angeles.
When I think of the people of that many states unknown, yet are
the places to decide an election.
I try to make a mental picture of a typical mid-western person
first, he is hard-working calls his father sir eager to help with
mechanical things around the house.
He tends to eat a lot, his mother always fed him well, making him
a strong young man
He is a Christian in the remarkable American way: Sure, I donate
to the church and believe in Jesus
He is conservative, a man thinks his country is the best in the
world (it is), and supports American intervention in the Far East,
based on the information he has
which are based on propaganda.
Living in the middle of America, he has been shielded from news
that has an alternative to his information, it takes a long time
to turn, when he does, you do get Trump.

Furry mice

Many years ago, I was in Houston (Texas) to victualize a new cargo ship, back then a ship carried a large crew for all the functions needed.

The ship chandler was keen to show me his enormous freezer, beef, mutton, pork, and chicken, he also sold horse meat, but not to the Nordic or the British for who eating horseflesh was akin to eating your relatives.

However, the Frenc, the Belgians, and the Dutch had no such hangups, as did ships with flags from eastern countries bothered by such sentiment.

He told me they had come over furry mice alive and well and breeding, I asked to see one of these creatures they had killed them- after all it- is- about vermin

I had a mental picture of them looking like aggressive but tiny polar bears biting my finger when I try to catch one of them, or look like black bears as long as they didn't look like rats.

Shipping in Norway was big business, employed about 50 to 60 thousand people, but when the flag was internationalized, seafaring history ended

In our time, modern ships are nearly fully automatic only a handful of computer readers are needed and for food, a drone delivers hamburgers with hot fries and soft drinks.

This is the ultimate goal of all industries to function without staff, selling goods to the unemployed?

Wishful

I can meet you in an open field
or a place where bombs fall
I shall be prepared
there is no one to blame but life itself
So quickly taken away like a switch on my night light
or failed brake in a car
I have a secret weapon
my memory will stretch until infinity
encompasses the galaxy and beyond because
I remember my birth
and the Stone Age
Nothing is forgotten, the brain is a computer
stores everything from the banal
to the sublime
From here to there, in the blink of an eye
You shall not defeat me

two islands

There was two islands, a big one and called
the new island, the other is small and called
On the old island, the pair was connected by a bridge.
I crossed the bridge to see my girlfriend, who lived
on the old island in a shack, all houses were shacks
The fishermen lived there in suitable poverty.
I knocked on the door that cracked, letting out
a good light, the steps to the house were
made of rough unfriendly stones.
Her mother opened I didn't like her smelling of beer
she had three teeth left and spoke like a whistle.
She hated me for being a cook at a tourist hotel
work she thought was for skulkers men with soft
hands incapable of doing a proper job, like fishing
Mackerel for a living.
She has gone with her new boyfriend on his boat
he is a skipper to Denmark and with that,
she slammed the door shut.
On the news, a bridge crossing Crimea to Russia
has been blown up; when I crossed the bridge to get
to the new island, I thought of doing something
similar, but having no knowledge of dynamite
I let it pass.

Pubs and restaurants can open soon
but schools must be shut
beer is more alpha than education
is not important apart

from reading and writing, the computer
does the rest and we can rest by the bank
of idiocy while watching a quiz
on the sainted TV

Our ignorance suits the elite, the poor
do not strike, but those with schooling do
they ask questions, are knowledgeable
and not easily impressed

The pandemic has made authorities
more potent than they dared hope before
for now, we do as we are told when the time
is right, we shall take our freedom back

The wrong side

He is old, lives behind tall walls, his garden is overgrown
Cats prowled for them a perfect suburban jungle.
As a national socialist, he had fought in the wrong
side of the war, and when the war ended, he was jailed
in a war, he thought the West lost
As a young man, he had gone to Russia, where hunger
killed thousands of people, land workers who
Had died of starvation
Vidkun Quisling, a major in the army, Quisling and him
Hated communism as evil.
The major, his friend, had been executed after the war
The old man, had spent several years in prison.
He sat in his garden with « the cat on his lap
it was a fine spring
The garden, full of new life and death.
Lately, the tide had turned, and the conservatives ruled.
Perhaps he should walk outside or write about
his views, but he hesitated, his views didn't matter
anymore had served his time, and that was it

A day of sunlight

Cascais has had a few good days with sunlight and no rain
already, the meteorologists are worried, interviewed on TV
They display concerned faces, and more rain is needed.
I used to live in the Algarve every year,
the story was about
the lack of rain "seca"
The idea was to bring water from the North, channel it
down to Algarve, but to do this, and since we live in a democracy
every Tom, Dick, and Harry's opinions have to be heard
if the day comes when tourists have to bring drums of water
there might be a consensus to stop farmers in Alentejo
" no digging of drains in our land."
Sometimes our cherished
democracy needs a little push.
Our planet has been subjected to many climate changes
perhaps we are in the middle of one now and have nothing
much to do with oil and gas production
society needs oil products like petrol, diesel, and coal
the battery car is a fancy idea grasped by those who know
how to turn a shilling; as for wind farms, we have to dot
the whole country, to the expense of farmland, to get
capacity, but still, it will not cover all the world's needs
when a lake or a dam runs dry, it is caused by ~hydro
electric, and not by the weather, and for those with eyes to see,
spring is more lush now than it used to be

Oil jack-boot

When coming home for vacation from his tank ship, the village
is in an uproar from every window; the people shouted and
banged pot pans together
People danced in the street, which was unheard of, and young
people shamelessly made love under oak trees so eagerly that
trees that had been around forever lost their leaves.
From the window, his mother hollered: we have
more money than the Americans, wealthier than the Saudis.
His father said, Son, no point going back to the sea
we are rich and get the Philippines to do the sailing bit
People had forgotten the socialist state had a word to say
The money made in this bonanza was for future use
put in a fond, and already rich could lend money, from this fond
and get richer.
For the plebs, there was little to gain, but for the professional
a disaster, the ship owners changed the flag and hired people
for a low-priced pay and no vacation
Goodbye Merchant Navy;
you served the owner class, the wealthy elite,
but we
the seaman, you abandoned

the visit

A knock on the door to my conscience
it was my brother, I hadn't seen for fifty years
while I have grown old, he has stayed the same
dark hair and pale, smooth facial feature
When I was young, he was loved by many as
he had a pleasant nature and was always willing to Help people
in need.
He had disappeared from us, for my mother
a shock, he was the memory of birth she gave
When she was young and in love.
He was worried about our sister, who she missed
her three children, although she had seen them
growing up, she was not happy with the way
they had turned, critical and darkness of mind
like their father, she could not make contact with
as he existed in a warmer climate, impervious
of fire, he was a helping hand in the kingdom
best avoided, a place where laughter is a grim
grin of laughter that sounded like a scream
My brother, since I was the oldest, wanted
to speak to her and press upon her other was
no way she could see them, but wait till they
one by one turned to her.
We spent an hour reminiscing about our
young years and he fatal fishing trip when
the strong current had grabbed and carried
him away from us
I had blamed myself for this tragedy and
had carried the burden of my guilt because

it was me who wanted to go fishing
No, it was not your fault for a reason we
cannot understand it was the time for me to go
before he left promised, that one day, we will
all be together again

The world of an elderly person

Lately, when going to the garage, open the door
to drive my car out into the street, I feel nervous
and unsure, asking myself questions about my
ability to drive that I might be past this simple
knowledge
Nervous translates into action hands are jerky
I drive and brake too often at the traffic lights,
hesitate, my hands are moist with sweat
I sit in a dark room, open and close, my fists with
ease, I get up off the chair, sit down, and get up
many times, my knees are bendable and hurt not.
Is this the end of the line sitting in the park; will
a kind person, help me to cross the road
The other day when I passed a man walking his
a dog that sensed weakness and animals are ready to kill the
weakest pray
The owner told the dog to be quiet, yet it's head and growled
once more
Dogs have no empathy nature, made them killers that, when
tamed, become man's trusted servant
there is a dance competition on the TV. I get up and dance in the
room and ask myself, why is that when outside, I lose my calm
and feel feeble

Another dimension

dimension has its center on the emotional side
of the brain, about not knowing what you know
except in certain circumstances when fractures
appear when the past and the future merge.
The authorities were looking for a sunken U-boat
using underwater drones, they found many things
A brig, sunk in a storm a luminosity of a lone figure
looking up and smiling before turning into watery dust.
A German U-boat surrendered, waving a white cloth
but such was the hatred, the boat was sunk anyway
They found the sub-marine missed it had a design
flaw when diving too steep an angle, the sub could
not rectify itself but kept going down.
They heard and didn't hear the scream of a young
realizing he should never know the sweetest love.
The fifth dimension is the moment when the past
and the present merge, everything is understood
clearly, but never spoken of

Carlson, the roofer

I know of a famous neuro-surgeon who retired at 65 to write a book that made him
more famous that is good for any ego
Now he is 72 and has cancer of the testicles,
life in the fast lane has ended.
In the night, he is visited by patients who died on his table or were left in a vegetive state,
This, I think, is caused by him performing surgery when he knew the outcome.
He tells the dead that he had followed procedure somehow. This sounds like "Following Order!"
is what the guilty of war crimes say.
He worries about getting old, decrepit
needing
a nurse to wipe his bum,
so undignified for a famous man.
When he visits his hospital where he reigned supreme, he is forgotten except for
the relic of a porter who salutes him, he is glad for that.
The newer generation sees him as another
old man, coming for his checkup and treating him
with hurried nonchalance.
Sic Gloria Mundi.

at the doctors

There are days when I feel bereft
the people I knew, are all dead
and no one is coming to take their place
there is a sense that I'm a waterlogged tree floating in a sullied
inland lake where bathing is prohibited
my nights are full of ghosts from the past visiting when
not awakened by nerve pains traveling up and down my legs
and the burning sensation telling of the eternal flames of hell
I'm sitting at the diabetic doctor's office complaining about
the depression of pain I suffer at night
the man has an ascetic face, a real doctor and not a product
of a mother's wish to have a son with the title
You are keeping your sugar level well-balanced, which is good
your weight is right! (at this point, I pull my stomach in
As for your discomfort, you have to see this as a part of your illness
I think he calls my pain DISCOMFORT!
He prescribes prescription for Insulin pens and tells me my blood
pressure
is perfect, with that he sends me away with a friendly slap
on my sagging shoulder

the war of the world

I have fought in many wars, mainly against the dark forces of my mind
this was a different war, and it happened in Falluja, where war crimes
were committed that will never be held responsible,
like the war crimes in Gaza, where the victims get the blame
There was an explosion in the basement of a factory, and I was flung
onto the floor, blood and dust screams from the wounded
When the US troops entered, they killed the wounded; this was not
a day to take any prisoners.
Of all the ironies in the world, I was wearing a NATO uniform
and saved
it struck me then, it still strikes me
what was a NATO soldier
doing in Iraq?
The slam to the floor had taken my breath away
a heart attack and carried to safety by a murderous soldier
suddenly being caring
after all, I was America's foreign army,
always ready
to go to war on the behest of the sainted USA
When I woke up in a Portuguese hospital, I tried to articulate what
had happened, they said I had been dreaming and gave
a sedative and told not to speak about this
any more people might
think I was crazy, so I kept this a secret until now.
I speak up now because of the mass slaughter of people in Gaza
we must stop these criminals from escaping their justice!

A strange lunch

Today, we drove in a taxi to the center of Cascais
because finding a parking place near where we were
going is frustrating.
with our official business done, it was time for lunch
an Italian cafe looked promising; the waiter came with
he was an Indian and spoke no Portuguese or English
we ordered something that sounded Italian and waited
and waited, finally we got four toasts with soft cheese
As we were hungry, we ate the toast, but when the bill
came, I protested
A beautiful Indian woman came out, and my heart melted
with lips that could tell no lies, proceeded
to tell a whopper
it was an Italian dish fused with Indian food.
Her husband came, he was slightly elderly and used a cane
a slight limp, it is possible he used to be a racing driver
I liked the way he touched wif's arm slightly
the Indians
do not demonstrate affection in public, which is nice
but next time when in town, I will stick to local dishes

Dark as Night

There is a sense of the déjà vu after a feast
life is not what we thought it was the banner of battle
no longer flies on top of the town hall.
The hero is not a hero but a figure fluctuating in the wind
and ruled by outside forces where he is only the visible
to fool the world into a shared vision of bravery.
There are so many other problems with the scourge of pest
the sizzling heat burning human skin crisp
and rain that kills and the sea that floods the landscape.
The undertone is getting louder; we have been lied to
dark forces seek a unipolar world, malleable people
into enslavement, where words are no longer truthful
but lies are endlessly repeated until the lies are the truth.
It is late in the day, but there is a rumble of a fightback
the freedom of the individual precariously wilts like
grains of life die if not rescued by the rain of revolt.

The Pope and Haute Culture

A pope has died, not the sitting one, but the one who loved wearing red hats,
style, silk dresses with intricate motifs of praying mantises
There he was, driving his VW on Holiday in the Swiss
when smoke, on a windless day, made him pope
A mild-mannered man took up the burden as
the role, of a saintly communicator of God's wishes.
He was an honorable man for a reason between him and God resigned.
Many things happened during the years, like the Haute Culture lady;
her dalliance with German officers,
during a fatal war, was forgotten,
and why not a lady have to survive
A low-ranking officer in the KGB ended up as president
in a social-democratic country, with an added touch of dictatorial,
made the Russians proud.
Did he wonder when he was a spy, it would come to this?
A very old man is the president of the USA.
His handlers tell him what to say
should he suddenly die, we have the pleasure of Kamala Harris and the courtesy of people
with two passports overseeing business; the mediocre tend to win the highest office
When it is New Year again, millions of people will
fill the streets for fireworks display; one gathers Gaza has had enough fireworks by now

Home, Jaimes

It is time to go home
to the village and the simple life
where I belong and everyone
my dog's name
and tourists are a rare sight.
Across the Alentejo on the plain
where horses gallop because
they enjoy the running
if it gets too hot, I can stop and rest
with sheep under a carob tree
I will take the long road home
the motorway is like driving in a roofless tunnel
If the journey is too long, I will stay
for a night at a rustic hotel
and leisurely be on my way
my house has been empty for too long
needs my company
and the dog's happy morning bark

Hot days

it is early, but the petrol station is open, where I can buy bottles of cold water
The heat is ominous and holds no promise of summer and fun, it is more like a door into hell left open. I hear the scream of those who are burning forever; one would think the screamers would be impervious to pain
I sit on a stone bench in the shadow of a tree
and dream of swimming naked in a lake of love
Naturally, the lake has dried up, as have the tributaries that came from the hazy mountain
No, not that one, but the one that had snow on top; it hits me with tremendous force
you are 85. What the hell do you expect of life?
Do they think I'm English? The way the locals stir at me when I sit on a cooling stone bench
it is normal to take my trousers off

Hot days

it is early, but the petrol station is open, where I can buy bottles of cold water
The heat is ominous and holds no promise of summer and fun, it is more like a door into hell left open. I hear the scream of those who are burning forever; one would think the screamers would be impervious to pain
I sit on a stone bench in the shadow of a tree
and dream of swimming naked in a lake of love
Naturally, the lake has dried up, as have the tributaries that came from the hazy mountain
No, not that one, but the one that had snow on top; it hits me with tremendous force
you are 85. What the hell do you expect of life?
Do they think I'm English? The way the locals stir at me when I sit on a cooling stone bench
it is normal to take my trousers off

the heritage

Should a person, say, a Christian, forgo his faith?
He can say Christianity means nothing to him
for most people, this is true, only they are deluding themselves
everyone born under a Western sky will soon see that
most things have religious context, even down to our thoughts
we use a thinking channel based on the scriptures in the bible
Thake books, most novels have a theme that is moral
we believe in sin and redemption
we also think the Ten Commandments address religious issues
to be free of Christianity is virtually impossible because
we cannot deny that faith is a part of us
Will you forgo your cultural heritage?

Furry mice

Many years ago, I was in Houston (Texas) to victualize
a new cargo ship, back then a ship carried a large crew
for all the functions needed.
The ship chandler was keen to show me his enormous
freezer, beef, mutton, pork, and chicken, he also sold
horse meat, but not to the Nordic or the British for
who eating horseflesh was akin to eating your
relatives.
However, the Frenc, the Belgians, and the Dutch had
no such hangups, as did ships with flags from eastern
countries bothered by such sentiment.
He told me they had come over furry mice alive and
well and breeding, I asked to see one of these creatures
they had killed them- after all, it- is- about vermin
I had a mental picture of them looking like aggressive
but tiny polar bears biting my finger when I try to
catch one of them, or look like black bears as long as
they didn't look like rats.
Shipping in Norway was big business, employed
about 50 to 60 thousand people, but when the flag
was internationalized, seafaring history ended
In our time, modern ships are nearly fully automatic
only a handful of computer readers are needed
and for food, a drone delivers hamburgers with hot
fries and soft drinks.
This is the ultimate goal of all industries to function
without staff, selling goods to the unemployed?

The Avenue

it is a delight to get up early
the days smell fresh, and the avenue is busy
with cars and buses looks rested and
the banks, nail bars, the yoga club too
and the hair salon appears coy.
These places are expensive and used by
The well-to-rich people
My wife uses a hairdresser in another street
and as for me, modest hair grows
she cuts my hair.
In our building, many people sleep until ten o'clock or more,
losing parts of the day.
I drink my coffee at the petrol station when dog owners are out
with their car
that used to bark at me, now they wagtails
as good morning.

Wishful

I can meet you in an open field
or a place where bombs fall
I shall be prepared
there is no one to blame but life itself
So quickly taken away like a switch on my night light
or failed brake in a car
I have a secret weapon
my memory will stretch until infinity
encompasses the galaxy and beyond because
I remember my birth
and the Stone Age
Nothing is forgotten, the brain is a computer
stores everything from the banal
to the sublime
From here to there, in the blink of an eye
You shall not defeat me!

the 1948 tragedy

Israel declared statehood, the West was happy
the Jews had suffered and deserved a state
the fact that 700 thousand Palestinians lost
their homeland was overlooked.
We were all pro-Israel back then and thought
the Jews would usher in peace and prosperity
it was not to be!
We see the Israel of hope has turned violent
it wants more Jordan, Lebanon, Syria, and they
appear unstoppable and protected by the USA
can overlook the world's disgust.
Because of Israel's intransigence, new groups
like Hamas and the Hezbollah are dedicated
to end this Hebrew death cult of Israel.
In power now are the Zionists, who are hellbent
sensing and killing everything in their way
The Palestine people (40 % cristians) have
suffered cruelly at the hands of those we came
from the devasted Europe to find a new life
alas, they also had hatred in their hearts
and, as always, the innocent pay the price.
We, the people, what can we do?
We can stop buyin Israelly product and stan
firm against those who tell us we are
anti-Semitic a stigma we must bear with
fortitude

An author

A woman I know writes books about suburban gardens
flowers and dulcet childhood memories, she says
her pussy stirs her to write about children; she is unmarried
I tried to emulate her success; in the street, I picked up
a likely moggy resisted and scratched me; a woman
came said it was her pussy, called me a thief.
Police were called, and I tried to with blood-dripping hands-
to explain it was a grave mistake I had wanted to caress
the confounded animals.
I finally got a tabby and began writing love poems
I had a modest triumph; this upset my cat feel
It was not apricated receiving tinned salmon and
full-fat milk, the tabby sent an email to the defense
Ligue for mistreated domestic animals.
I banished the moggy to the garage where it could
catch mice, no computer and mobile phone, and went
back writing about doom and gloom.

the cook and his sister

once I was a poet blinded by the shiny pebbles, by the shore
of purity and heart delight, but it was not to be
although it was said about me in India, this man is really innocent
My sister stood crying at the railway station in Montreal
so, what's the tears for are you not alive
you silly girl ; I have been dead for 44 years
and you think you i have forgotten
can forget about real life, anyway
I have never been
in Montreal, especially now that I'm dead
you should see the main street in Montreal
it is the longest
in a world with hundreds of shops and cafes, you can get
Borch in seven variations, alas their sons became lawyers
now it is Mcdonald's burgers and Indian curry houses
What has that got to do with my worries
I have never been
here before and wants to go home to my sons, if they have
not forgotten me; take me home brother!
Shells fell from my eyes, and I stood naked as a statue in
a graveyard with no footsteps in the snow, oh, you silly man
when are you going back to what you knew, a drunk cook
on sunken ships

The Wanderer

His marriage was of the middle-class type
the house bought years ago had trebled in value
which his wife liked to point out.
Of course, few people actually own a house
as they pay the mortgage, ownership is an illusion.
He was an average man with a good job, lived
a good life, fucked his wife every Saturday night
after drinking wine when the loins stirred.
He was not happy but sad, thought life
had a better thing to offer and walked away.
Through towns and villages, he wandered to find
the elusive that gave existence meaning.
A quiet man, which many think is profound
when it is bewildering, the lack of grasping
the fatality of the truth.
He walked through many lands and saw rebellions
that didn't register as he looked inward like
He was blind; when he finally stopped walking
lived in a hut, he realized life was boring.

www.ingramcontent.com/pod-product-compliance
Ingram Content Group UK Ltd.
Pitfield, Milton Keynes, MK11 3LW, UK
UKHW041316190726
13845UKWH00025B/311

9 789363 541962